REDEEMED
from
POVERTY

Receiving God's Promise of Provision and Prosperity

Bill Winston

Redeemed from Poverty: Receiving God's Promise of Provision and Prosperity

Copyright © 2023 by Bill Winston

Published by HigherLife Publishing & Marketing, Inc.
PO Box 623307
Oviedo, FL 32762
AHigherLife.com

Unless otherwise indicated, Scriptures are taken from the King James Version of the Bible.

Scripture quotations marked TLB are taken from *The Living Bible*. Copyright © 1971. Used by permission of Tyndale House Publishers, Inc., Wheaton, IL 60189. All rights reserved.

Scripture quotations marked GNT are from the *Good News Translation in Today's English Version—Second Edition*. Copyright © 1992 by American Bible Society. Used by permission.

Scripture quotations marked TPT are taken from *The Passion Translation*®. Copyright © 2017, 2018 by Passion & Fire Ministries, Inc. Used by permission. All rights reserved. ThePassionTranslation. com.

Scripture marked EXB are taken from *The Expanded Bible*. Copyright © 2011 by Thomas Nelson. Used by permission. All rights reserved.

Cover and Interior Design by Faithe Thomas, Master Design Marketing, LLC

ISBN (Paperback): 978-1-954533-57-8

ISBN (Ebook): 978-1-954533-58-5

Library of Congress # 1-10890092181

Printed in the United States of America.

Contents

Introduction vii

1. A Covenant of Blessing 1

2. The Law and the Curse 13

3. Redeemed from the Curse 27

4. Heirs of the Promise 37

5. God Does Not Want His People Poor 45

6. Spiritual Warfare 59

7. Inheriting the Earth 75

Conclusion 89

Prayer for Salvation 92

Prayer for the Baptism of the Holy Spirit 93

Scripture References 94

William (Bill) Samuel Winston 95

Books by Bill Winston 97

Connect with Us! 99

Introduction

THERE IS NO MORE important subject in the Christian faith than the reality of redemption—the subject of this book. Redemption goes way beyond your eternal salvation. It actually covers every area of life here on earth before you get to heaven.

In *Redeemed from Poverty: Receiving God's Promise of Provision and Prosperity,* we will examine God's promise in the Bible for you to have a long, satisfying life that will be a blessing not only to you but also to your family, community, and beyond.

Let's start with the definition of *redeemed,* which means "to be brought back or bought back." We were in captivity, but we've been brought out of that captivity.

In *Redeemed from Poverty: Receiving God's Promise of Provision and Prosperity,* you will learn how:

- The Blessing of Abraham is for you today.
- You are an heir of God's promise to inherit the earth.

- God does not want His people to be poor or in debt.
- God has given you spiritual armor to defeat satan's army.
- Your faith can call in an abundant harvest.

As a born-again believer, you have been redeemed from poverty. You are no longer limited to the economic and cultural problems of this world system because you are operating in the new economy of the Kingdom of God that cannot fail. In this Kingdom, you have access to power, provision, and protection that the world knows nothing about.

> **Christ hath redeemed us from the curse of the law, being made a curse for us: for it is written, Cursed *is* every one that hangeth on a tree: that the blessing of Abraham might come on the Gentiles through Jesus Christ; that we might receive the promise of the Spirit through faith.**
>
> —Galatians 3:13–14

You are a joint heir with Jesus Christ and the seed of Abraham. With this knowledge, you have the ability to manifest both spiritual and material blessings in your

life: "For the promise, that he should be the heir of the world, was not to Abraham, or to his seed, through the law, but through the righteousness of faith" (Romans 4:13).

It is important to know that you do not have to work for these blessings. They have been freely given to you through the covenant of God. Just walk in them!

CHAPTER 1

A Covenant of Blessing

I N THE BEGINNING, EVERYTHING God made was good, including His man, Adam, who was created in the image of God. What happened to change all that? You know the story: Adam sinned, and because he sinned, death passed to all men. The resulting curse was passed down to all humanity. It was loosed into the earth!

Though disobedience brought an end to the unlimited blessings and communication with their Creator for Adam and his wife, Eve, in the Garden of Eden, God was not finished blessing His beloved creation.

A man named Abram (Abraham) entered the scene.

Now the Lord had said unto Abram, Get thee out of thy country, and from thy

kindred, and from thy father's house, unto a land that I will shew thee: and I will make of thee a great nation, and I will bless thee, and make thy name great; and thou shalt be a blessing: and I will bless them that bless thee, and curse him that curseth thee: and in thee shall all families of the earth be blessed.

—Genesis 12:1–3

Here God was saying, "I want you to come out from your dependence on this world system and its economy and its way of doing things. Come on out of there." That was Abram's part. "And I will make of you a great nation. And I will bless you, and make your name great." Whose part is that? It's God's part!

"And thou shalt be a blessing." So you and I have two parts in this mandate from God: to come out of the world system and then to be a blessing.

You Are Blessed to Be a Blessing

I found this out in my own personal life and ministry. God's going to make my name great; He's going to bless me—and God has fulfilled that! I did exactly what He said. I came out of the system I was in. Now, this doesn't

necessarily mean you run out and quit your job, but it does mean you should come out of dependence on the world's economic system.

When God called me into the ministry, it was at a time when I didn't have much. We had spent all our money and moved to Chicago with about $200 in our pockets and no place of our own to stay. God is faithful! A dear sister opened up her home, and we stayed with her for about eight months, which enabled us to get the ministry started.

The Blessing Empowers You to Get Wealth

Abraham started his journey not knowing where he was going, but he trusted God to lead him. So, in my own life and ministry, I began to track the Blessing of Abraham, and it tracks right on through the generations to this very day. The Blessing that God put on Abraham empowered Abraham—and will empower you too—to get wealth.

A Lesson to Learn

Let's pick up the story in Genesis 12:4: "So Abram departed, as the Lord had spoken unto him; and Lot went with him: and Abram was seventy and five years old when he departed out of Haran."

Lot turns out to be a problem. We need to learn from this because many of us are trying to take folks with us who are not really with us. I won't say any more about that, but note what Genesis 12:9–10 said: "And Abram journeyed, going on still toward the south. And there was a famine in the land: and Abram went down into Egypt to sojourn there; for the famine was grievous in the land."

Note that the famine wasn't grievous down there in Egypt; the famine was only grievous in the land God showed him. Sometimes, God will show you a land that is in shortage, that is needy, that is hurting. He will direct you to things that are going to cause you to think, "Wait a minute! Is this the Lord?

God Is Gracious

Abram went down to Egypt, and this is my paraphrase of what he told his wife, Sarai (later Sarah): "Now tell

them you're my sister because you know you look pretty good, girl. Don't tell them you're my wife because they might want to kill me to get hold of you." Sarai must've looked very good, even though she was probably in her mid-sixties by this time. You know, Pharaoh wasn't going to have anything in his house that was marginal.

Abram didn't exactly follow God in telling his wife to say that. (Thank God for His grace and patience with us!) Despite this, watch what happened next: "And Abram went up out of Egypt, he, and his wife, and all that he had, and Lot with him, into the south. And Abram was very rich in cattle, in silver, and in gold" (Genesis 13:1–2).

And Abram was what? Very rich! Genesis 13:2 in the Amplified Bible says, "Now Abram was extremely rich in livestock and in silver and in gold." The Blessing of Abraham is on you to get gold.

Unusual Blessings of Riches

Not only was Abram rich, but his nephew Lot also had great wealth. "And Lot also, which went with Abram, had flocks, and herds, and tents. And the land was not

able to bear them, that they might dwell together: for their substance was great, so that they could not dwell together" (Genesis 13:5–6).

Strife Enters the Picture

"And there was a strife between the herdsmen of Abram's cattle and the herdsmen of Lot's cattle" (Genesis 13:7). Now what does the Bible say about strife in James 3:16? "For where envying and strife is, there is confusion and every evil work."

Confusion makes it so you can hardly hear God: "I don't know what God wants me to do…. I don't know what God wants me to get." You know why you can't hear God? You've got strife! Strife will keep you from accessing your promised land and prevent you from receiving all God wants to give you.

Now, we've seen movies about Abraham out there keeping those little sheep, but that's not the picture I'm getting. I'm seeing that he's got enough for a whole country!

You've Got to See It to Take Hold of God's Blessings

Understand this: you can't go any further than you can see. If the enemy can paint the wrong picture inside, you'll end up receiving the wrong thing, so you've got to get the revelation: "This man is rich!" Abram was very rich, extremely rich, but strife entered the situation, so Abram said, "Listen, Lot, whatever you want, you take it. If you go to the right, I'll go to the left. If you go to the left, I'll go to the right." Why could Abram say that? Because he had The Blessing on his life. Anywhere Abram went, he knew he would prosper.

> And Lot lifted up his eyes, and beheld all
> the plain of Jordan, that it was well watered
> every where, before the Lord destroyed
> Sodom and Gomorrah, even as the garden
> of the Lord, like the land of Egypt, as thou
> comest unto Zoar. Then Lot chose him all
> the plain of Jordan; and Lot journeyed east:
> and they separated themselves the one from
> the other.
>
> —Genesis 13:10–11

The problem in this is Sodom and Gomorrah. That was the only place in the Bible on which God rained down fire and brimstone, destroying the whole place. It looked good at first but, you know, everything that looks good is not always good for you.

Pursuing the Enemy

While Lot was living in the land he chose, the enemy came down, took Sodom and Gomorrah, took the kings, took the people, took their possessions, and led them off into captivity. "When Abram heard that his nephew [Lot] had been captured, he armed and led out his trained men, born in his own house, [numbering] three hundred and eighteen, and went in pursuit as far [north] as Dan" (Genesis 14:14 AMP).

This is what I want you to get: Abram had 318 servants with him that were born in his house. If they were born in his house, they each had a mother and a father. Some of them were probably married and had their own children, so there could be two thousand or more people there in Abram's camp.

Get this picture: This thing was pretty big. This man was getting blessed. Abram pursued the enemy and

whipped them. He smote them. He slaughtered them. "And he brought back all the goods, and also brought back his nephew Lot and his possessions, and also the women, and the people" (Genesis 14:16 AMP).

A Covenant Is Ratified in Blood

In Genesis 15, the covenant between God and Abram was ratified. It shows the importance of the shedding of blood that we see later in the "once for all" sacrifice of Jesus Christ. (See Hebrews 10:1–10.)

> **And [God] said unto [Abram], Take me an heifer of three years old, and a she goat of three years old, and a ram of three years old, and a turtledove, and a young pigeon. And he took unto him all these, and divided them in the midst, and laid each piece one against another: but the birds divided he not....And when the sun was going down, a deep sleep fell upon Abram; and, lo, an horror of great darkness fell upon him....And it came to pass, that, when the sun went down, and it was dark, behold a smoking furnace, and a burning lamp that passed between those pieces. In**

> **the same day the Lord made a covenant
> with Abram, saying, Unto thy seed have
> I given this land, from the river of Egypt
> unto the great river, the river Euphrates.**
> —Genesis 15: 9–10, 12, 17–18

This was when they ratified the covenant on God's side. Abram's part came in chapter 17 when he was circumcised. Each one of these was a token (or a sign) of the covenant God made with Abraham. It was an everlasting covenant made not only for Abraham but also to his seed. So technically, when the covenant was made, Christ was there because there is no time in God.

You've Got The Blessing on Your Life

If you're born again, you've got The Blessing on your life. **Say, "I've got The Blessing."** What did this blessing do for Abraham? We already saw this in Genesis 13:1–2: "And Abram went up out of Egypt, he, and his wife, and all that he had, and Lot with him, into the south. And Abram was very rich in cattle, in silver, and in gold."

So, The Blessing of Abraham will get you some cattle, some silver, and some gold. Now here's the unique thing about this that's key. People don't have a problem with being rich—what they have a problem with is God doing it. As long as they work three jobs, long hours, lose their families, have their kids running wild, and so on, they don't have a problem. But what about if you work normal hours, go home, spend quality time with your kids, love your spouse, and still get rich, not because you did it but because God did it? Does that bother you?

I'm not coming against people. It's the world system that dictates that kind of thinking. They don't understand God's economy; but praise God, you and I do, and we're going to live in it!

CHAPTER 2

The Law and the Curse

As we learned in the last chapter, God made a covenant with a man named Abram, whom He brought out of a place called Ur of the Chaldees, where people were making and worshiping idols. Understand that up until that time, mankind had many gods, but now God Himself was calling a man out to serve the one true living God. This was unheard of during that time. Even today you can go into nations like India and others that practice Hinduism and see their millions of gods and goddesses—there's one for everything.

So now, God was calling Himself the God of Abraham. He's in three persons: Father, Son, and Holy Ghost, but He's still one God. I want you to see this because this was different. Not only was Abraham called

to serve one God, but he was also called to serve a God he couldn't see. Further, he recognized that this God is all powerful. He's the Most High God, the El Elyon.

Four hundred thirty years after God's covenant with Abraham was established, a man named Moses was called to lead the children of Israel out of their captivity in the land of Egypt. God used Moses to deliver the captives. They spent forty years in the wilderness, and the people had become very sinful, making themselves a golden calf and returning to idol worship.

The Law Enters In

God gave Moses the Ten Commandments to give to the people. Many other laws were added through the years as well. Why was the Law added? Galatians 3 gives us the answer:

> **Why, then, the Law [what was its purpose]?**
> **It was added [after the promise to**
> **Abraham, to reveal to people their guilt]**
> **because of transgressions [that is, to make**
> **people conscious of the sinfulness of sin],**
> **and [the Law] was ordained through angels**
> ***and* delivered to Israel by the hand of a**
> **mediator [Moses, the mediator between**

**God and Israel, to be in effect] until the
Seed would come to whom the promise had
been made.**

—Galatians 3:19 AMP

What are transgressions? Sins! People missing God. They were so sinful that God added the Law, but it says here that if the covenant was made, the Law could not undo it. The covenant of Abraham was made around 645 years *before* Moses brought the Law in. When the Law was added, it was added because of transgressions until the Seed should come.

Where the Spirit of the Lord Is, There Is Liberty

Who is the Seed? Christ. The Mosaic Law was in place until Jesus came, but once Jesus came, the Law said, "Oops! My time is up," and it walked off. In fact, we learn that the Law wasn't even meant for a righteous person: "Knowing this, that the law is not made for a righteous man, but for the lawless and disobedient, for the ungodly and for sinners, for unholy and profane, for murderers of fathers and murderers of mothers, for manslayers" (1 Timothy 1:9).

The Law is simply a tutor for us until we receive Christ. "Now the Lord is that Spirit: and where the Spirit of the Lord is, there is liberty" (2 Corinthians 3:17). God wants us to be led by His Spirit for we, as born-again Christians, are the sons of God. *The Expanded Bible* says this: "Everything God made [The creation] is waiting with excitement [eager expectation] for God to show his children's glory completely [the revelation of the children/sons of God]" (Romans 8:19). And this is not meant to take anything away from women: sons simply refers to mature offspring.

God Is Restoring Righteousness

God is restoring righteousness. One of the reasons Jesus came is to restore us to our former state. But from the beginning until the present day, satan has always tried to separate us from our Creator and His original plan.

Satan's strategy is to keep us ignorant, keep us in unbelief, keep us religious, and keep us sin conscious, which has to do with the condemned state Adam fell into when he sinned in the Garden. God came looking for Adam, who hid himself from God.

That's what happens when sin consciousness is operating: People cannot receive from God as they should. Sin consciousness keeps us in bondage and fear, and subject to an inferiority complex. In other words, instead of feeling like we rule over everything, it seems as if things are ruling over us, such as weed, drugs, alcohol, pornography, and every evil practice known to man.

The price for sin has already been paid through Jesus—which we'll learn more about in the next chapter—but the devil wants us to think we have to pay it again and again and again. Satan brings sickness, poverty, and brokenness to people, who say, "I'm suffering for the Lord." You're not suffering for the Lord! The devil's trying to kill you! He wants to keep us working in his system and getting no benefit out of it.

Righteousness Comes through Faith Alone

Man's inability to keep the Law in his own strength shows the absolute need for God's grace. God's promises are not based on our being perfect, because if they were, none of us would survive. His promises and

blessings are based on our faith—believing what God said in His Word.

Real faith comes in when righteousness returns. The Bible says this: "Beloved, if our heart condemn us not, then have we confidence toward God" (1 John 3:21). In other words, if there's condemnation in your heart, your faith won't work.

A Better Covenant

Before Jesus came, people were dependent on keeping the Law for their righteousness, and there wasn't much they could do about it. Jesus hadn't come yet to give man back the authority he lost in the Garden. Many times people think they are limited to what they see in the Old Testament. This is not true because as born-again believers we have a new covenant, the New Testament. We have a better covenant with better promises. Praise God!

For example, you cannot find an instance anywhere in the Old Testament in which a person could cast out a demon. Why? Because they didn't have the spiritual authority to do that—until Jesus came and restored the authority God originally intended man to have. When

Jesus was resurrected, we were restored to God's mandate to have dominion over all things in the earth.

A Higher Economic System

In God's Kingdom, there is a higher economic system. God showed this to me through the story of Joseph in the Old Testament and gave me this pattern for our Joseph Center ministry. Joseph ran the most powerful economy in the world. As second-in-command in Egypt, Joseph's system prospered, saving not only Egypt but also his family and the children of Israel. Meanwhile, in all the neighboring nations, there was economic collapse.

Have you ever thought about why Joseph went through being sold as a slave and thrown into prison? He had to be transferred out of his tribal setting into a place where the mechanism of The Blessing of Abraham could operate in him. God may move some of you too, if it's necessary to position you where you can be fruitful and do great things for His Kingdom. The Blessing of Abraham is on you. **Say, "The Blessing of Abraham is on me, and I am blessed!"**

The Blessing Is Not Automatic

I want to share with you how the blessed can be cursed. The first way is by the words that are spoken over you. Even though The Blessing of Abraham is on you, it is not automatically triggered. You've got to follow God, and He'll lead you to a place where the mechanisms are there to trigger The Blessing of Abraham in your life. If you've got The Blessing on your life, you can go to a place that's barren and it'll come out looking like the Garden of Eden.

Look What The Blessing Did!

When we came to the Forest Park Plaza, the mall God told me to buy, there wasn't anything there. I mean, there were hardly any retail businesses in this mall— just a bunch of empty, barren storefronts, but look at what The Blessing did. Everybody said it was a failed mall, but now it's operating at full capacity with profitable retail stores, restaurants, salons, and even a bank.

Now that's not something that has just happened once in my life. When I was working at a computer company, I got saved and began studying faith and following people who taught faith and how to live by it all

the time. I learned how these blessings are manifested and soon had an opportunity to put my faith into practice.

The company gave me a sales territory that I didn't think was quite equitable. By the time I left that particular position people were fighting over that territory. Why? Nobody thought anything was in that territory, but they saw I had The Blessing on my life.

Not only that, but when I got to be a first-line manager, they gave me some folks to manage. Because I was new in the office, they gave me the least productive folks. And guess what? I became the number one marketing manager in the organization.

Do you hear what I'm saying? God can move you into something where everybody else has failed, but if The Blessing is on your life, you will be the one who succeeds!

Negative Words Can Curse You and Rob Your Blessing

As I said earlier, the first way the blessed can be cursed is by negative words being spoken over a person or situation. Remember the story of Jacob, who tricked his

brother Esau out of his birthright and had to flee for his life? He ran to his uncle Laban's house and married both of his daughters.

Having worked for Laban for many years, Jacob decided it was time to take his two wives, their livestock, and their belongings, and return to his father's house. You can find the story in Genesis 31.

Verse 19 says, "Rachel had stolen the images that were her father's." When accused of stealing, Jacob, who was unaware of what had happened, said this, "With whomsoever thou findest thy gods, let him not live: before our brethren discern thou what is thine with me, and take it to thee. For Jacob knew not that Rachel had stolen them" (Genesis 31:32).

Jacob said that, didn't he? Now, let's look at Genesis 35:

> And they journeyed from Bethel; and there
> was but a little way to come to Ephrath:
> and Rachel travailed, and she had hard
> labour. And it came to pass, when she was
> in hard labour, that the midwife said unto
> her, Fear not; thou shalt have this son
> also. And it came to pass, as her soul was
> in departing, (for she died) that she called

**his name Benoni: but his father called him
Benjamin. And Rachel died.**

—Genesis 35:16–19

What do you think was one of the reasons Rachel
died? Because of what Jacob unknowingly spoke over
her life.

Watch What You Say

People today say all kinds of things they wouldn't want
to come true, such as, "My feet are killing me." Don't
speak words like these over yourself—or others! You
can even curse your own son or daughter by what you
say over them. "Ah, you're not going to amount to anything! Watch! You're going to be just like your daddy!"

As a believer, you've got a right to call things that be
not as though they were and God gets involved! (See
Romans 4:17.)

The Bible says in Proverbs 6:2 that "thou art snared
with the words of thy mouth, thou art taken with the
words of thy mouth." Or as it is rendered in the Con-
temporary English Version: "Then you are trapped by
your own words."

Generational Curses Can Cause The Blessing Not to Work

The next thing that can rob you of your blessing is a generational curse. Generational curses come through family lines, often through deceased (or living) relatives who have spoken curses over people, sometimes through practicing witchcraft or sorcery. You can break generational curses with your own words.

Say this with me: "Father, in the Name of Jesus, every word that has been spoken against me, against my family, or against my future—right now, I sever it from my life. I loose myself from every hex, vex, spell, jinx, psychic power, bewitchment, witchcraft power, or sorcery that has been sent out against me or my family line back to ten generations. I loose myself and my family from it now in Jesus' Name! I cut it off with the blood of Jesus. Your Word says that whoever the Son sets free is free indeed! I'm free! My children are free! My spouse is free! My relatives are free! In the Name of Jesus, we are free indeed!"

The System of Tithing Brings Blessings or Cursings

Another thing that can cause the blessed to be cursed is robbing God of the tithe. The tithe opens up supernatural heavens over your life so that you'll never be broke another day in your life.

> Will a man rob God? Yet ye have robbed
> me. But ye say, Wherein have we robbed
> thee? In tithes and offerings. Ye are cursed
> with a curse: for ye have robbed
> me, even this whole nation. Bring ye all
> the tithes into the storehouse, that there
> may be meat in mine house, and prove me
> now herewith, saith the Lord of hosts, if I
> will not open you the windows of heaven,
> and pour you out a blessing, that there
> shall not be room enough to receive it. And
> I will rebuke the devourer for your sakes.
>
> —Malachi 3:8–11

We'll go more into the history of tithing in a later chapter and answer controversial questions about this very important topic that is so consequential to the effective working of The Blessing in your life.

CHAPTER 3

Redeemed from the Curse

IN THE OLD TESTAMENT there's an interesting passage that sheds light on how Jesus Christ would later redeem us from the curse.

> **If someone has committed a crime worthy of death and is executed and hung on a tree, the body must not remain hanging from the tree overnight. You must bury the body that same day, for anyone who is hung is cursed in the sight of God. In this way, you will prevent the defilement of the land the Lord your God is giving you as your special possession.**
>
> —Deuteronomy 21:22–23 NLT

When people had sinned a sin worthy of death, they were hung on a tree. You couldn't let them stay there all night. You had to take them down and bury them the same day. Curses came inside that particular person if he were left hanging on the tree, and the land would be defiled.

This was a foreshadowing of what would happen to Jesus when He was crucified and put on the cross. Remember the sign they put over Jesus? It said, "King of the Jews." This carried with it the idea that all the curses would come into Jesus, their Messiah.

They took His body down before the night had ended, just as directed in the passage above. Jesus received all the sin, sickness, and pain, and every curse into Himself. This is how you and I go free! The Amplified Bible, Classic Edition puts it this way:

> **Surely He has borne our griefs (sicknesses, weaknesses, and distresses) and carried our sorrows and pains [of punishment], yet we [ignorantly] considered Him stricken, smitten, and afflicted by God [as if with leprosy]. But He was wounded for our transgressions, He was bruised for our guilt and iniquities; the chastisement**

> **[needful to obtain] peace and well-being for us was upon Him, and with the stripes [that wounded] Him we are healed and made whole.**
>
> —Isaiah 53:4–5 AMPC

And we know that Jesus wasn't killed by the authorities. He could have called legions of angels to protect Him, but He didn't. He simply "gave up the ghost" (Luke 23:46). Why? For you and me and everyone who will believe and receive all that Christ paid for on that cross. If you are born again, you don't have to fear being punished or try to make up for your sins—Christ already did it for you! Praise God!

You Have Been Redeemed from the Curse

God sent One called a Redeemer, and His Name is Jesus.

> **Christ hath redeemed us from the curse of the law, being made a curse for us: for it is written, Cursed is every one that hangeth on a tree: that the blessing of Abraham might come on the Gentiles through Jesus**

**Christ; that we might receive the promise of
the Spirit through faith.**

—Galatians 3:13–14

Read part of that again: "Christ hath redeemed [put
your name in here] from the curse of the law, being
made a curse for [put your name in here too]." That's
really what happened—Jesus Himself became a curse
for us. Let's read on down in this chapter to verse 15:
"Brethren, I speak after the manner of men; Though it
be but a man's covenant, yet if it be confirmed, no man
disannulleth, or addeth thereto."

And then, verse 16 says, "Now to Abraham and
his seed were the promises made. He saith not, And
to seeds, as of many; but as of one, And to thy seed,
which is Christ."

Verse 17 reiterates that the covenant cannot be un-
done or made void: "And this I say, that the covenant, that
was confirmed before of God in Christ, the law, which
was four hundred and thirty years after, cannot dis-
annul, that it should make the promise of none effect."

When Man Broke the Law of God, a Curse Entered the Earth

As I said earlier, a curse came on the earth because of mankind's sin. This was the result of breaking the law of God. Though God told him not to eat of the tree, Adam ate of it; and because of that, a curse came into this earth and sin passed upon all men.

God knew we couldn't save ourselves by keeping the Law—"If you obey every law except one, you are still guilty of breaking them all" (James 2:10 CEV)—so He sent Jesus, the last Adam, to redeem us.

Redeemed means "being bought back, being returned to our former state, returned to where Adam fell from." How did Jesus redeem us? Jesus redeemed us by His blood: "In whom we have redemption through his blood, the forgiveness of sins, according to the riches of his grace" (Ephesians 1:7).

God's undeserved grace has been poured out upon mankind. Jesus didn't come to condemn the world. He didn't come to condemn us because we were condemned already. (See John 3:16–19.) But He gave His life, the Bible says, as a ransom for many. Jesus Himself gave His life so that you and I could be saved, so

we could come back to God, come back to that place that Adam had occupied before he committed his act of treason.

Only You Have the Power to Hold You Back

The devil is through. I said the devil is through! And do you know what? He has no power. For the believer, he has been stripped of all power. The only power he has is the power you give him. He doesn't even have the power to hold you back from being a millionaire, and he cannot take you out of this earth. Look what Romans 12:1–2 says:

> **I beseech you therefore, brethren, by the mercies of God, that ye present your bodies a living sacrifice, holy, acceptable unto God, which is your reasonable service. And be not conformed to this world: but be ye transformed by the renewing of your mind, that ye may prove what is that good, and acceptable, and perfect, will of God.**

Note that verse 2 urges this: "And be not conformed to this world." To be *conformed* means "to be fashioned

or pressured into the world's mode or the world's way of doing something." We must not let ourselves be pressured into the world's ways.

See, you've got to get that revelation in your mind. You've got to renew your thinking. *Renew* means more than changing the conscious mind. The conscious mind is always busy just figuring things out in the here and now, but the subconscious mind is where 95 percent of your mental activity comes from. The only way to renew your subconscious is through meditation—through a spiritual experience.

That's why they run commercials over and over again. Repetition is one way to change the subconscious. You see the same commercial again and again: "Have a Coke, have a Coke, have a Coke, have a Coke, have a Coke, have a Coke." Then you go to the grocery store, and you end up over there in the Coke aisle because the world has programmed you to go there and buy one.

What You Bind on Earth Is Bound in Heaven

You're going to have to put something else in your mind that will overcome the enemy's strategies. He shows us movies in which satan has all the strength and power. Some monster comes along, and it always has more power than the people.

This is not true! God says this: "Verily I say unto you, Whatsoever ye shall bind on earth shall be bound in heaven: and whatsoever ye shall loose on earth shall be loosed in heaven" (Matthew 18:18). You ought to be able to step back if a monster comes near you and say, "I bind you in the Name of Jesus Christ!"

Those movies are not showing you the power you have to bind and loose. They are trying to indoctrinate you. They're trying to reinforce an image that satan has power. He doesn't have power over the believer. Remember, satan is under your feet!

It's Time You Step on the Devil

Come on, step on the devil a little bit! Step on him! That's what you've got to do! You've got to remind yourself that satan has no power over you! "Behold, I

give unto you power to tread on serpents and scorpions, and over all the power of the enemy: and nothing shall by any means hurt you" (Luke 10:19).

I like the way the Passion Translation says it: "Now you understand that I have imparted to you my authority to trample over his kingdom. You will trample upon every demon before you and overcome every power Satan possesses. Absolutely nothing will harm you as you walk in this authority."

Don't be cowardly and shrink back, saying, "Ooh, maybe I shouldn't have said that." Say it again! Bind every demonic spirit that is trying to steal, kill, and destroy your life or the lives of your loved ones. Realize that the devil is trying to keep himself in your life by deceiving and intimidating you!

Recognize the Strategies of Satan

Satan's strategy is to keep us ignorant of what we have been redeemed from and what we have been redeemed to. His plan is to keep people paying for their sins through their own efforts, to keep people suffering, and to keep people basically working the world's system, barely existing day to day, trying to make it in life.

Through His Word and by His Spirit, God has given us the knowledge and the understanding that we've been redeemed from the curse, and that "the blessing of Abraham might come on the Gentiles through Jesus Christ; that we might receive the promise of the Spirit through faith" (Galatians 3:14).

CHAPTER 4

Heirs of the Promise

A S WE CONTINUE TRACING The Blessing of Abraham through the Word of God, we've looked at all we've been redeemed from. We've been redeemed from poverty, we've been redeemed from sickness, and we've been redeemed from death.

In this chapter, we will find out what we are redeemed into, who can get it, and how to access it. To begin, let's review: "Now to Abraham and his seed were the promises made. He saith not, And to seeds, as of many; but as of one, And to thy seed, which is Christ" (Galatians 3:16). As believers, we are in Christ and He is in us, so are we eligible to receive the promise of the Spirit? Yes!

Look at the first chapter of the book of Acts where Jesus commanded His disciples thus: "Wait here for

the Father to give you the Holy Spirit, just as I told you he has promised to do" (Acts 1:4 CEV). Then the Holy Spirit was given to the followers of Jesus, and they were baptized into Him.

Who Is Abraham's Seed?

If the covenant and God's promise were made to Abraham and his seed, does that mean they are only for Jews? Here is what the Scripture says:

> **For as many of you as have been baptized into Christ have put on Christ. There is neither Jew nor Greek, there is neither bond nor free, there is neither male nor female: for ye are all one in Christ Jesus. And if ye be Christ's, then are ye Abraham's seed, and heirs according to the promise.**
> —Galatians 3:27–29 emphasis added

We are heirs of what? Heirs according to the promise. Praise God! The promise that God made Abraham is the same promise you get if you're in Christ.

You get the same promise. Now, you need to find out what God promised Abraham and what He didn't promise him. Understand that God did not promise

Abraham spiritual blessings because in Abraham's time, he couldn't receive the spiritual blessings since he was not born again. What does this mean? The Blessing of Abraham is a material blessing.

Spiritual Blessings Come through Christ

The spiritual blessings were granted when Christ came. In Christ, the new covenant was cut, making it possible for us to receive the spiritual blessings. In the Old Testament, we are talking about The Blessing of Abraham—the riches of gold, livestock, land, and so forth, that Abram possessed, as we discovered in the first chapter of this book.

You Must Have Faith to Receive the Promise of the Spirit

Right after Galatians 3:13 tells us that Christ redeemed us from the curse, verse 14 says that "the blessing of Abraham might come on the Gentiles through Jesus Christ; that we might receive the promise of the Spirit *through faith*" (emphasis added).

How does faith come? By hearing—hearing the Word of God! If you haven't heard the Word of God concerning whatever promise or blessing you desire from God, then faith is not there. If faith is not there, you can't receive the blessings. We've been talking about blessings—plural—here, but there's something bigger and better: The Blessing.

Now, don't put an *s* on The Blessing because that's not what it is. It is The Blessing. Singular. It is one blessing, and out of that one blessing you get multiple blessings. That one blessing is an anointing, and it's through that anointing that you can receive *all* the other blessings that are available to you in God's Word.

One note here: Let's back up to the scripture I quoted in verse 14. It said "might." It didn't say "will." This means if you're not obedient and don't walk in faith, the blessings won't come—even though it is God's will to bless you.

God's Promise of the Spirit

I repeat: For you to get the promise of the Spirit, you're going to have to have some faith. Well, let's just see what that promise is: "For the promise, that he should

be the *heir of the world*, was not to Abraham, or to his seed, through the law, but through the righteousness of faith" (Romans 4:13 emphasis added).

I want you to see this clearly. What is the promise? The promise is that Abraham is going to be the "heir of the world"! The Living Bible adds another degree of clarity: "It is clear, then, that God's promise to give the whole earth to Abraham and his descendants was not because Abraham obeyed God's laws but because he trusted God to keep his promise."

The Amplified Bible, Classic Edition says it this way: "For the promise to Abraham or his posterity, that he should inherit the world, did not come through [observing the commands of] the Law but through the righteousness of faith."

God is promising Abraham that he will inherit the whole earth here. He promised to give him the whole world, but that promise wasn't to Abraham only.

You've Become an Heir of the World

Speaking about Abraham in Romans, we see that "all them that believe" receive the promise to become heirs of the world. Here's this section in fuller context:

And he received the sign of circumcision,
a seal of the righteousness of the faith
which he had yet being uncircumcised:
that he might be the father of all them that
believe, though they be not circumcised;
that righteousness might be imputed unto
them also: and the father of circumcision
to them who are not of the circumcision
only, but who also walk in the steps of that
faith of our father Abraham, which he
had being yet uncircumcised. For the
promise, that he should be the *heir of
the world*, was not to Abraham, or to his
seed, through the law, but through the
righteousness of faith.

—Romans 4:11–13 emphasis added

Restoring Kingdom Rule to God's People

The term *heir of the world* means "to inherit the world." If you remember, Adam had been given charge of the world in the first place: "And God blessed them, and God said unto them, Be fruitful, and multiply, and replenish the earth, and subdue it: and *have dominion*

over the fish of the sea, and over the fowl of the air, and over every living thing that moveth upon the earth" (Genesis 1:28 emphasis added).

Because of his sin, Adam lost that dominion for all mankind. But there's good news! Jesus came to demonstrate the truth to us and change and rearrange things in the earth. He came to restore Kingdom rule to God's people. However, first He had to get God's people back to God. How? Jesus came preaching the gospel of the Kingdom to seek and save that which was lost.

No Sickness, Poverty, or Lack

Once we come back to the Kingdom of God and into God's family, then we need to get back what we have lost or was stolen from us—everything that is due us! The prophet Joel said, "And I will restore to you the years that the locust hath eaten" (Joel 2:25).

Jesus instructed His disciples (and that includes all believers today) to pray in this way: "Thy kingdom come, thy will be done in earth, as it is in heaven" (Matthew 6:10). I ask you, what are things like in heaven? There is no sickness, no poverty or lack, no sadness, no pain and suffering. Why? God wants you to have

heaven on earth. It is not His desire or plan for you to be poor: "I alone know the plans I have for you, plans to bring you prosperity and not disaster, plans to bring about the future you hope for" (Jeremiah 29:11 GNT).

CHAPTER 5

God Does Not Want His People Poor

D O YOU REMEMBER THE story in the Bible about Isaac and Rebekah? Abraham is very old and sends his servant to his homeland to find a wife for his son Isaac from among his relatives. The servant goes to the land of Nahor, where he meets a beautiful girl named Rebekah at a well. She gives him a drink and waters his camels. This fulfills the criteria the servant had asked of God.

Abraham's servant goes back with Rebekah to her father's house and says, "I *am* Abraham's servant. And the Lord hath blessed my master greatly; and he is become great: and he hath given him flocks, and herds, and silver, and gold, and menservants, and maidservants, and camels, and asses" (Genesis 24:34–35).

When you convert those assets into today's environment, they become transportation systems, banks, and much more. In other words, Abraham was a very, very wealthy man.

"And Abraham gave all that he had unto Isaac" (Genesis 25:5). Note that Abraham not only gave Isaac two thousand people, and gold, silver, and cattle—he also gave him The Blessing, The Blessing of Abraham! He passed on The Blessing that was on him to his son Isaac.

The Blessing Is Passed On

Watch what happens to Isaac, who now has The Blessing: "And there was a famine in the land, beside the first famine that was in the days of Abraham. And Isaac went unto Abimelech king of the Philistines unto Gerar" (Genesis 26:1). Next, the Lord appeared unto him, and said, "Don't go to Egypt."

Look how the next couple of verses read in the Living Bible: "Jehovah appeared to him there and told him, 'Don't go to Egypt. Do as I say and stay here in this land. If you do, I will be with you and bless you, and I will give all this land to you and to your descendants,

just as I promised Abraham your father'" (Genesis 26: 2–3 TLB).

See, God led Isaac again to a land that was experiencing a severe shortage. He led him there on purpose! He said, "Don't leave this land now. It's easy to go to Egypt, but don't go. Stay where I put you."

God's Blessings Are Going to Overtake You

Abraham and Isaac were obedient to God's instructions. God is no respecter of persons. The Blessing will operate in your life too, if you do what God says in His Word:

> **And it shall come to pass, if thou shalt hearken diligently unto the voice of the Lord thy God, to observe and to do all his commandments which I command thee this day, that the Lord thy God will set thee on high above all nations of the earth: and all these blessings shall come on thee, and overtake thee, if thou shalt hearken unto the voice of the Lord thy God.**
>
> —Deuteronomy 28:1–2

Now, note that this says, "If thou shalt hearken" to God's commandments. He's not talking about the Ten Commandments, because we are no longer under the Law. This is speaking of anything God tells you to do. It becomes His commandment to you.

And get this, *His commandments are not grievous.* He's not going to tell you to run a 26.2-mile marathon in Chicago or climb Mt. Vesuvius. His commandments are not grievous. Folks, they are not hard. He just said, "Stay in this land."

God Saw Something I Didn't

Now, what happened to me? I was minding my own business, and leading services in the Chez Roué Banquet Hall in Forest Park, Illinois. God brought me outdoors and said, "See that mall over there? Buy it." I thought I was hearing things. I looked at the mall, which had already been bought and sold twice. Each buyer had tried to revive it, but it was still dead. Here was God leading me to something that looked impossible!

After a while I said, "Oh, okay." I followed Him because The Blessing is on me, and it's on *you* in the

same way! That's what I'm trying to get across to you. It's on every one of us! "If ye be Christ's, then are ye Abraham's seed, and *heirs* (Galatians 3:29). You've got that blessing on you right now! For what? For gold! For silver! For cattle! For property! For businesses! You've got it on you right now!

We've got to stop speaking the wrong words. Our words have been used against us. You've been saying, "Well, nobody can do anything with that." Well, maybe they can't do anything with that, but *you can* do something with it because *God is with you!* The anointing to get wealth is on you!

You can go into anywhere! People are going to offer you businesses, or God's going to tell you to buy one that has gone down in the dumps; they look like they're gone and shot! They look like there's nothing that can be done with them. But God will guide you. In my case, God said, "Buy that." And when God shows you that business, I decree that in one year's time, you're going to turn a billion-dollar profit!

You Can Be Delivered from Lack

What I'm trying to do is get past your unbelief.

Look at this scripture with me: "For there is no difference between the Jew and the Greek: for the same Lord over all is *rich* unto all that call upon him" (Romans 10:12 emphasis added). *Rich* means that He is generous and bestows riches upon all that call upon him: "For whosoever shall call upon the name of the Lord shall be *saved*" (Romans 10:13 emphasis added).

In the Greek, *saved* means "healed, preserved, made whole, and delivered"—and that includes deliverance from lack, debt, and having just enough for you, your four, and no more. What you need to do is stand flat-footed right where you are and *declare*: **"This day shall the Lord's deliverance come into my life!"** Say it out loud right now.

You've got The Blessing on your life. Your race, your education level, your financial status, where you live, or anything else about you can't stop The Blessing from working unless you let it. Acts 10:34–35 says: "Then Peter opened his mouth, and said, Of a truth I perceive that God is no respecter of persons: but in every nation he that feareth him, and worketh righteousness, is *accepted with him*" (emphasis added).

Notice the phrase *accepted with him*. It means that everyone who fears God and does righteousness has the *same* access to God's promised blessings.

You Have Access to His Blessings

"Well, I'm from Africa, we don't have...." "I'm from Haiti, we don't have...." Wait a minute! It doesn't matter what your background or circumstances are. God can use you to manifest The Blessing of Abraham because He's no respecter of persons.

We saw The Blessing passed on from Abraham to Isaac. Now it's time for that same blessing to be passed on to Isaac's son, Jacob:

> **And Isaac called Jacob, and blessed him,
> and charged him, and said unto him....
> And God Almighty bless thee, and make
> thee fruitful, and multiply thee, that thou
> mayest be a multitude of people; and give
> thee the blessing of Abraham, to thee, and
> to thy seed with thee; that thou mayest
> inherit the land wherein thou art a stranger,
> which God gave unto Abraham.**
>
> —Genesis 28:1, 3–4

See how The Blessing has been passed on from generation to generation? It goes all the way to you if you are in Christ!

Is the Truth Making You Free?

Understand this: The enemy is trying to cause people in the Church to wrongly divide the Word and stay in bondage as a result. Folks, if I'd been on the road to Mississippi for forty years and hadn't gotten there yet, something would be wrong. I would have to be on the wrong road.

Truth is the Word of God, but you have to *continue in it*, not just read about it. John 8 declares, "If ye continue in my word, then are ye my disciples indeed; and ye shall know the truth, and the truth shall make you free" (John 8:31–32).

If you've been sitting in church and you're still broke, something's wrong. If you've been sitting in church and you're still sick, or you're still hurting, or your marriage is still in trouble, or you are still having problems with your kids, *you're on the wrong road*. You don't have the truth.

The truth is not making you free because you haven't got hold of it. You've got hold of something, but you don't have hold of the truth.

God Will Permit What You Permit

I'm here to tell you right now that there is a permissive will and a causative will of God. God will permit some things. What will He permit? He'll permit what you permit.

Look at Adam. He told Adam, "Don't eat of the tree." Didn't He tell him that? Did God permit Adam to eat of it? Yes, He did! What I'm saying is this: God will allow what you allow.

Here is a key scripture that you must understand: "Thy kingdom come, Thy will be done in earth, as it is in heaven. Give us this day our daily bread. And forgive us our debts, as we forgive our debtors. And lead us not into temptation, but deliver us from evil" (Matthew 6:10–13).

God doesn't want you to even be tempted by satan. This is why He said to pray that you would not be tempted by the devil. God's got better things for you

to do than for you to sit all day being tempted by the devil.

Work Brings Out Your Potential

This world's fallen system brought us into a place where we had to labor for everything we got. After Adam's sin in the Garden was exposed, God said to him, "You will have to work hard and sweat to make the soil produce anything, until you go back to the soil from which you were formed. You were made from soil, and you will become soil again" (Genesis 3:19 GNT).

The whole concept of a job came from the Babylonian world system. You work a job to earn a paycheck. It's different if you're going to get some seed, but you're getting a paycheck. Seed and a paycheck are two different things.

There's also a difference between a job and work. Work is something designed to bring out your potential. God gave Adam work, not a job! There isn't any real empowerment that comes from a job. Empowerment comes from work when you take on the attitude of an entrepreneur.

You see, I can work or be working for somebody and get the money. Then I can sow a seed with that money and buy a three-flat crosstown, rent it out, and that three-flat is going to work for me while I'm sleeping! That's a big difference.

Work comes from the Greek word *ergon*, which has to do with energy. You work along with God, and the potential that's in you begins to come out. Your work brings out your gift, and your gift will make room for you and bring you before great men!

A Wealth Transfer Is Coming from God

God is going to transfer the wealth out of the hands of the wicked into the hands of the righteous. The wealth belongs in the Church for the spreading of the gospel. The world needs to know what Jesus did for them. "For ye know the grace of our Lord Jesus Christ, that, though he was rich, yet for your sakes he became poor, that ye through his poverty might be rich" (2 Corinthians 8:9).

This scripture says you *might* be rich. You might be rich, and you might not be if you don't receive what He did for you. The enemy is not going to put that

money in your hands voluntarily. The devil will fight you tooth and nail to keep you from leaving his system and his way of thinking.

This worldly economy that we're looking at here was birthed by man. It is not of God because it left all the important things out. Man left out the Holy Ghost, the blood, the Name, and morality. You can make money in the world's system by putting up nothing but gambling casinos—but not in God's kingdom!

This is the way you're going to have to get the money: "And from the days of John the Baptist until now the kingdom of heaven suffereth violence, and the violent take it by force" (Matthew 11:12). Now, you can't go out and stick somebody up; that's not what he's talking about. As we covered before in Galatians, "the blessing of Abraham might come on the Gentiles through Jesus Christ; that *we might receive the promise of the Spirit through faith*" (Galatians 3:14 emphasis added).

Faith Takes for the Sake of the Gospel

Faith takes! Take everything you need! Strip the wealthy, ungodly elites. There's no way that you're supposed to tolerate some of the ungodly things that are

going on. The Bible says the rich rule over the poor and the borrower is servant to the lender. That means it is impossible for us to rule in this human system without financial empowerment.

God made it so you can't do it. "Remember that it is the Lord your God who gives you the power to become rich. He does this because he is still faithful today to the covenant that he made with your ancestors" (Deuteronomy 8:18 GNT).

He never intended for you to preach His gospel being broke. God intended for you to have some money, and I'm not just talking about millions. I'm talking about the gospel that He wants to preach. It will take billions to do that, and guaranteed, He's going to put it in somebody's hand.

The wealthiest man in the world is not going to be in the Old Testament. Old Solomon had it all. I know he did, but the Bible says in the New Testament that someone greater than Solomon is here! (See Matthew 12:42.) It says that the glory of the latter house is going to be greater than the former house! (See Haggai 2:9.)

God says this: "The gold and the silver are Mine; the cattle on a thousand hills are Mine!" (See Haggai 2:8

and Psalm 50:10.) These resources don't belong to the devil or anybody ungodly! It doesn't matter what credentials or status they've got. If they're ungodly, they're on the other side, and they're going to be stripped!

CHAPTER 6

Spiritual Warfare

When I was a sales manager in computers, I worked my faith. The economy was down, and the managers were going to lunch and having a pity party every day. We'd talk about how bad everything was and how the company was not treating us right. We'd repeat that the economy was really down, and continually talk about how the company was still requiring all of this work from us, and on and on and on.

One day God got hold of me and said, "What are you doing?" I said, "Well, I'm talking about how bad it is." He said, "Why don't you use your faith? Why don't you use what you've been teaching?" What a wake-up call! So, I began to call things that were not as though they were. One day my sister called me, asking how

business was, and I said, "Call me back this afternoon, and I'll have more business than we can put on the books."

That day I hadn't just started out with zero sales; I started out with a minus! By the end of that day, I had so much business that my manager said, "Bill, we can't put all this on the books. Let's save some of this for next month." Not only was there enough business for me, but there was enough for the whole office!

Get the principle here: **This blessing that we've been talking about is designed to go into places that look bad, beat up, in the red, and suffering—like nothing can be done for them. That may be true for the person trying to make it on their own, but not for you. Why? You've got the anointing to get wealth!**

If you've got The Blessing of Abraham in your life, God will often lead you to a place of severe shortage, and He'll lead you there because that is the mechanism that He needs for The Blessing to manifest! There's gold in this city! There is silver in the "hood"! It might look like a poor area, but there's gold in there!

It Looked like a War Zone

When my wife and I started our ministry in Chicago, God sent me to Lake and Pulaski Streets. There I was—used to white shirts and dark pinstriped suits and so forth—stepping into the roughest neighborhood in the city at that time! That place looked like a war zone. It might be better now, but then, we had to sweep up whiskey bottles before we could even walk in the door. But you know what? God sent us there, and we packed the house out!

People Are Not Your Source

Then God moved us out of Chicago to a nearby suburb, Forest Park, Illinois. Half the people from the city didn't want to go. They said, "No, we're not called to Forest Park."

I said, "Called? You're going where I'm going, aren't you?"

Well, they stayed there, and I went to Forest Park. I said, "Lord, what am I going to do now? I've got rent and all these bills to pay, and all I have is a few people."

And God said something to me: "Well, who are you looking at?"

You see, we tend to look to people. People are not your source. He said, "Come out from among them! Depend on Me! Stop depending on people! Stop depending on your salary! Start depending on Me, and I will meet every need you've got!" And He has done just that!

It's Time to Grow

Do you remember the story of Joseph? His brothers sold him as a slave, and later he was put in prison for a crime he didn't commit. In the end, God promoted him to be second-in-command over all of Egypt. Why did he have to go through all that? It was because Joseph was too much "fish for his tank." He had to be transported to the place where God would use him.

There's this Japanese fish called a koi, and it has an interesting quality. Koi are limited in their growth by their environment. When a koi is in an environment where it can grow larger, it looks like a giant goldfish with whiskers. If you put him in a little fish bowl, he'll grow about three inches. Amazingly, you can take that same fish and put him in a large aquarium, and he'll grow about a foot! And if you put that fish in a lake,

he'll grow to be three feet or more! Jumbo varieties in a good-sized pond get to be larger still!

Is there somebody reading this book that fits this description? You've been looking for a little old fish bowl? You don't need a fish bowl; you need a sea! God's got big potential in you, and somehow you've been letting people hold you back. Get where God's called you to go! Do what He's called you to do. Life may look bad right now, but when you start calling things that are not as though they were, and see The Blessing of Abraham kick in, you'll be full of joy! Is there anything too hard for God?

Are you feeling like you're out of your comfort zone? God might want to move you into something bigger! Praise God! It's time to grow!

The enemy will try to keep you in that little fish bowl by making you feel condemned or as if you're not good enough. This is why he's always trying to remind you of everything you did wrong. The devil wants to condemn you so your faith won't work. Don't let him! He knows it's through faith that you'll receive God's blessings. If you are in Christ, you have The Blessing of Abraham operating in your life!

Satan Deceived the Whole World

You've got to renew your mind because the enemy has come in with deception. He couldn't stop you from being saved, but now he's trying to stop you from the reality of your redemption. He's trying to keep you from realizing what God has done for you in your life.

Revelation 12:9 says, "And the great dragon was cast out, that old serpent, called the Devil, and Satan, which deceiveth the whole world: he was cast out into the earth, and his angels were cast out with him." Realize this: if you are in the world, you were deceived.

One of the Greatest Apostles in the Bible Was Deceived

A person can be deceived and not even know it. We need light. People don't know they're deceived until the light comes and shows them. Paul, one of the greatest apostles of all time, was deceived. There's nothing worse than a man who's deceived and doesn't know it, because he'll fight you to stay where he is. He'll dig in where he is.

Let's read about Paul, whose name was changed from Saul:

> **And Saul, yet breathing out threatenings
> and slaughter against the disciples of
> the Lord, went unto the high priest, and
> desired of him letters to Damascus to the
> synagogues, that if he found any of this way,
> whether they were men or women, he might
> bring them bound unto Jerusalem.**
>
> —Acts 9:1–2

Men or women of the "way" refers to practicing Christians. Can you see Paul and his men binding and hauling people out of their homes to be imprisoned and tried? Some of them would be killed because they were serving Jesus! How horrible!

> **And as he journeyed, he came near
> Damascus: and suddenly there shined
> round about him a light from heaven: and
> he fell to the earth, and heard a voice saying
> unto him, Saul, Saul, why persecutest thou
> me? And he said, Who art thou, Lord?
> And the Lord said, I am Jesus whom thou
> persecutest: it is hard for thee to kick
> against the pricks. And he trembling and
> astonished said, Lord, what wilt thou have
> me to do? And the Lord said unto him,**

**Arise, and go into the city, and it shall be
told thee what thou must do.**

—Acts 9:3–6

Prior to this moment, Paul thought he was right in what he was doing. Even today, there are people like this in leadership positions in the Church. As soon as somebody like me starts preaching, they say, "He's one of those prosperity preachers," because they think they're right! But I'm here to tell you what the Word of God says: "Let them shout for joy and be glad, who favor my righteous cause; and let them say continually, 'Let the Lord be magnified, who has pleasure in the prosperity of His servant'" (Psalm 35:27 NKJV).

You've Got to Get a Revelation

God is the One who set up the rules. We cannot detect who satan is except by the Holy Spirit and the Word of God. However, you can't just *read* the Word of God; you've got to have a revelation of what God is saying! Deliverance from deception and every evil work of the enemy comes from God: "The righteous cry, and the Lord heareth, and delivereth them out of all their troubles" (Psalm 34:17).

Understand this: God isn't against prosperity. It takes finances to operate in His kingdom and fulfill His mandate for believers to take care of the earth. What God's against (and you and I should be too) is when wealth is used for the ungodly purposes of the wicked.

The Wealth Is in the Wrong Hands

Psalm 73 shows this clearly in two separate places: "For I was envious at the foolish, when I saw the prosperity of the wicked" (Psalm 73:3); and "Behold, these are the ungodly, who prosper in the world; they increase in riches" (Psalm 73:12).

Jesus referred to this also in the story about the unjust steward "because he had done wisely: for the children of this world are in their generation wiser than the children of light" (Luke 16:8). What was Jesus saying? He was saying that the money was in the wrong hands, which is a dangerous thing because they can do wicked things with it.

Who Is It That's behind the Evil?

We don't fight against people. Here is the real enemy: "How art thou fallen from heaven, O Lucifer, son of the

morning! how art thou cut down to the ground, which didst weaken the nations!" (Isaiah 14:12).

This Lucifer, who is now satan, was the anointed cherub that covered the throne of God, who raised himself up to be God. God put him out, and one third of the heavenly host (angels who are now demons) followed him.

Note what weakens nations in that verse: it's satan! "For thou hast said in thine heart, I will ascend into heaven, I will exalt my throne above the stars of God: I will sit also upon the mount of the congregation, in the sides of the north" (Isaiah 14:13).

Satan goes on with his boasting: "I will ascend above the heights of the clouds; I will be like the most High" (Isaiah 14:14). Pride comes before a fall and satan, as well as his kingdom of darkness, is about to come crashing down:

> **Yet thou shalt be brought down to hell, to the sides of the pit. They that see thee shall narrowly look upon thee, and consider thee, saying, Is this the man that made the earth to tremble, that did shake kingdoms; that made the world as a wilderness, and**

**destroyed the cities thereof; that opened
not the house of his prisoners?**

—Isaiah 14:15–17

I'm here to tell you who is behind the destruction of our cities. It's not people—it's satan. Who is behind making the world a wilderness? It's satan.

The Money Is Coming Back

The wealth has been in the wrong hands. You know, money doesn't make you sin; it just amplifies what you've got in you. It can be used for good or evil. "A good man leaveth an inheritance to his children's children: and the wealth of the sinner is laid up for the just" (Proverbs 13:22).

Who is this wealth laid up for? Us! The righteous. Now, the sinner is gathering it together, but he's not supposed to keep it. The Bible says if he keeps it, he's going to vex you with it. (See Numbers 33:55.)

What are the wicked doing with the wealth? Buying and producing drugs, committing crime, and the like—that's what. Look at what kids are watching on TV or the internet. It's all about sex and violence. When you try to write a letter to the Federal Bureau

of Communications about it, they do not respond! It's because satan is managing that whole system. But remember this: we're in the Kingdom. We're not here to take sides; we're here to take over! We're going to get it all back—the money, the property, and the people who have been deceived by satan. That's our mandate.

What did God promise to His people if they hearkened diligently to His voice? He said He would set them high above all nations of the earth and they would be the head, not the tail. They would be above, not beneath. They'll be the lender and not the borrower! (You can read all of the blessings God promised in Deuteronomy 28:1–14.)

As we've seen in much of this chapter, satan is out to steal all that God has provided for you in His kingdom: "The thief comes only in order to steal and kill and destroy. I came that they may have and enjoy life, and have it in abundance [to the full, till it overflows]" (John 10:10 AMP).

Be Strong in the Lord

A trick of the enemy is to try to get you to trust in your own ability. If he ever does get you to do that, he's

got you! Your ability is not enough to stop him. God hasn't called you to wage war against the devil and his demons in your own strength: "Finally, my brethren, *be strong in the Lord, and in the power of his might*" (Ephesians 6:10 emphasis added).

God has not left you without any armor to protect yourself, your loved ones, and your property. The Word of God describes this armor in detail in Ephesians: "Put on the full armor of God, so that you can take your stand against the devil's schemes" (Ephesians 6:11 NIV).

Note the next verse: "For our struggle is not against flesh and blood, but against the rulers, against the authorities, against the powers of this dark world and against the spiritual forces of evil in the heavenly realms" (Ephesians 6:12 NIV).

Our problem is not people—it's the demonic spirits that are using those people. That's what we're wrestling against. Why? Because satan is working overtime to keep the ungodly holding on to your money. For you to get in there, you're going to have to have the truth. Only the truth is going to make you free!

The Full Armor of God

The armor of God consists of both offensive and defensive weapons:

> Put on the full armor of God, so that you can take your stand against the devil's schemes. For our struggle is not against flesh and blood, but against the rulers, against the authorities, against the powers of this dark world and against the spiritual forces of evil in the heavenly realms. Therefore put on the full armor of God, so that when the day of evil comes, you may be able to stand your ground, and after you have done everything, to stand. Stand firm then, with the belt of truth buckled around your waist, with the breastplate of righteousness in place, and with your feet fitted with the readiness that comes from the gospel of peace. In addition to all this, take up the shield of faith, with which you can extinguish all the flaming arrows of the evil one. Take the helmet of salvation and the sword of the Spirit, which is the word of God. And pray in the Spirit on all occasions with all kinds of prayers and requests. With

**this in mind, be alert and always keep on
praying for all the Lord's people.**
—Ephesians 6:13–18 NIV

If you want to walk in the fullness of your redemption from poverty, you will find yourself engaging in spiritual warfare. But here's the good news about that: God has called us to win every battle with the armor He's provided.

CHAPTER 7

Inheriting the Earth

THE KINGDOM OF GOD restores people's lives. Jesus came to demonstrate the proof of what God said and bring the power of the Kingdom of God to change and rearrange this earth and people's lives. He also came to restore the Kingdom rule.

When I say *restore* I mean *re-*. *Re-* is a powerful prefix. It means "to do something again or to go back to its original state." For example, Joel 2:25 says, "And I will restore to you the years that the locust hath eaten."

When God says "restore," He's not referring to your life alone. He is going to restore you all the way back to what Adam had when Adam was first created. As we learned in chapter 4 of this book, God's promise to Abraham and his generations up to you and me today is that those who are in Christ shall inherit the world.

Adam had dominion over the world God created. Then, because Adam disobeyed God and sin entered the earth, satan took charge of this world. Jesus came to announce that "the kingdom of heaven is at hand" (Matthew 4:17), and now God is putting the world back into the hands of His family.

All Things Are Yours

Remember this: "Therefore let no man glory in men. For all things are yours" (1 Corinthians 3:21). We can see this also in 1 Corinthians 2:12: "Now we have received, not the spirit of the world, but the spirit which is of God; that we might know the things that are freely given to us of God."

All things are yours—God has given the earth to you. "The heaven, even the heavens, are the LORD's: but the earth hath he given to the children of men" (Psalm 115:16).

This means that whatever belongs to God belongs to me. Whatever belongs to Jesus belongs to me. I and my Father are one. Do you get what I'm saying? God has put you and me here to be stewards over this earth.

Poverty is a curse. Father God does not want any of His children to be poor. He has provided this earth with wealth and riches. It is abundantly supplied. He has provided all the resources we'll ever need for us to be rich. So wealth is in the earthly realm. God is restoring this earth to its rightful owners, His children, through a supernatural wealth transfer.

Inheriting the Earth

In the Sermon on the Mount, Jesus said, "Blessed are the meek: for they shall inherit the earth" (Matthew 5:5). What did Jesus say they would inherit? The earth! And the next verse says, "Blessed are they which do hunger and thirst after righteousness: for they shall be filled" (Matthew 5:6). This is saying that the righteous in God—that includes you and me—shall be filled!

"Ye are the salt of the earth," Jesus continued later in the same message (Matthew 5:13). He told His disciples this then, *and it's still true now*. What does salt do? It preserves whatever it's put in. We are supposed to preserve the earth and what's in it. Whatever satan did wrong, you can undo.

Where he put affliction on somebody, you can lay hands on them in Jesus' Name and they will be healed. Wherever the devil has caused a community to be dilapidated and destroyed, you can come in there with The Blessing of Abraham on your life and rearrange the whole thing. You can effect real change over any devastation.

A New Economic System

There is a new economic system available called the Kingdom of God, but it's not being taught because it has no probability! It has no economic cycles like man's economy does. Jesus taught about it, but the leaders were blind and didn't receive it. The leaders, He said, were blind leaders of the blind. If the blind lead the blind, what's going to happen to them? All of them are going to fall into a ditch!

It's the same today. I'm not saying anybody's doing it on purpose, but the whole world is deceived, as it says in Revelation 12. That doesn't leave anybody out. I don't care how many economic forecasts they make; if they don't know Jesus, they will not have the wisdom and ability to make any good and lasting change.

An economic collapse is coming! When it comes, you'll still be on top and it won't shake you at all because you're not part of the system that is about to be judged! You are in the Kingdom of God. The things of this world will get more and more ungodly, so God can't let it go on! It's got to be judged! God is not trying to destroy people's lives. He came to save them!

You Have a Role to Play in the End Time

Understand this: It's not the judgment of God. It's not the wrath of God. The judgment is coming from the system. God put a law in place that says that if you sow to the flesh you'll reap corruption. (See Galatians 6:8.) That's why the tsunamis are happening; that's why the earthquakes are getting more frequent. You can see biblical prophecy being fulfilled on the evening news. It's wrapping up, saints.

This is not a gloom and doom story—this is good news. *This is our time!* You're going to be able to preserve the earth! You are the Josephs! You are the Esthers! You've been made for such a time as this! You're

going to provide the jobs! You're going to have the plans! You're going to have the wisdom!

Remember, you are redeemed from poverty and lack and shortage. Even when others are struggling to survive in the times to come, you will have plenty, not only for yourself and your family, but enough left over to help others. What a testimony to the goodness of God!

Planting Seed for an Abundant Harvest

God has given us the keys to unlock prosperity even in the worst of times.

In chapter 1, we talked about how Abram and his trained servants pursued the enemy that had captured his nephew Lot and all his people and property. Abram was victorious: "And he brought back all the goods, and also brought back his nephew Lot and his possessions, and also the women, and the people" (Genesis 14:16 AMP). What happened next?

> **Then after Abram's return from the defeat (slaughter) of Chedorlaomer and the kings who were with him, the king of Sodom went out to meet him at the Valley**

of Shaveh (that is, the King's Valley). Melchizedek king of Salem (ancient Jerusalem) brought out bread and wine [for them]; he was the priest of God Most High. And Melchizedek blessed Abram and said, "Blessed (joyful, favored) be Abram by God Most High, Creator and Possessor of heaven and earth; and blessed, praised, and glorified be God Most High, who has given your enemies into your hand." And Abram gave him a tenth of all [the treasure he had taken in battle].

—Genesis 14:17–20 AMP

The King James Version of that last verse says it this way: "And blessed be the Most High God, which hath delivered thine enemies into thy hand. *And he gave him tithes of all*" (Genesis 14:20 emphasis added).

Tithing Is a Law of Prosperity

Abram gave tithes, meaning ten percent of what he had gotten in the fight, which is called spoil. He took the spoil back and gave it to the priest. Now, this happened before the Law. That means God instituted the practice of tithing before the Law of Moses came into effect.

Even earlier than this, in Genesis 4, you will see that Cain and Abel each brought an offering to God. Who taught them to do that? They had to have learned it from their daddy. Tithing started in the Garden!

Somebody may say, "Well, I thought tithing was under the Law." Tithing existed before the Law, but God put it under the Law so that His people could get the benefits of it. Tithing is a law. It's a law of prosperity. It's a way for God to release supernatural power and blessing into His people's lives.

Someone else may say, "Well, I'm struggling to make ends meet. I'll start tithing when things are better," or "I'm living paycheck to paycheck. I can't afford to tithe." The truth is that if you are struggling financially, you can't afford not to tithe! Tithing is the one thing in the Bible that God said we could test Him on (Malachi 3:10). Tithing is about trusting that God can do more with 90 percent than you can do with 100 percent. It is a spiritual discipline. So if you are struggling financially, start giving that first 10 percent back to God, and just watch what He does.

Cursed with a Curse

Remember, we are talking about being redeemed from poverty. You are using your faith to call in those things that belong to you. We know also that faith without works is dead. Look at what it says in Malachi 3:

> **Will a man rob God? Yet ye have robbed me. But ye say, Wherein have we robbed thee? In tithes and offerings. Ye are cursed with a curse: for ye have robbed me, even this whole nation. Bring ye all the tithes into the storehouse, that there may be meat in mine house, and prove me now herewith, saith the Lord of hosts, if I will not open you the windows of heaven, and pour you out a blessing, that there shall not be room enough to receive it. And I will rebuke the devourer for your sakes.**
>
> —Malachi 3:8–11

You have a choice to be blessed or cursed. In this scripture God says plainly, "Ye are cursed with a curse." Why? Because the people didn't bring their tithes and offerings into the House of God. Today that is the Church. What does God mean when He says people

are cursed? Basically, He's saying, "I've made a way for you to get under an umbrella of protection, and it's called the tithe; but if you refuse to tithe, you come out from under My protection and you're out there where the curses are."

Tithing is a covenant connector. It's not a burden—it's a benefit to you. It's a way God releases the supernatural in your life. Abraham tithed, and he was blessed abundantly with cattle, silver, and gold. Malachi 3:10 promises a blessing so great that you won't even have room to receive it. Praise God!

A Story of More than Enough

Faith and obedience unlock the door to prosperity. Look at the woman whose kids were about to be taken as slaves because her husband had died and left them in debt. Let's pick the story up here:

> **The wife of a man from the company of the prophets cried out to Elisha, "Your servant my husband is dead, and you know that he**

revered the Lord. But now his creditor is
coming to take my two boys as his slaves."

Elisha replied to her, "How can I help you?
Tell me, what do you have in your house?"

"Your servant has nothing there at all," she
said, "except a small jar of olive oil."
—2 Kings 4:1–2 NIV

Note that the first thing Elisha asked the woman
was, "What do you have in your house?" A miracle
starts with a seed. The widow's seed was her olive oil.
The man of God gave her instructions on what to do
next.

Elisha said, "Go around and ask all your
neighbors for empty jars. Don't ask for just
a few. Then go inside and shut the door
behind you and your sons. Pour oil into all
the jars, and as each is filled, put it to one
side." She left him and shut the door behind
her and her sons. They brought the jars to
her and she kept pouring.
—2 Kings 4:3–5 NIV

The little bit of oil she had was supernaturally multiplied, filling up one jar after another. This lady didn't know anything about oil or commodities. She just kept pouring and doing what the prophet told her to do.

> **When all the jars were full, she said to her son, "Bring me another one."**
>
> **But he replied, "There is not a jar left." Then the oil stopped flowing.**
> —2 Kings 4:6 NIV

Now, she had all these jars full of oil but didn't know what to do with them. This widow was undoubtedly not a business lady. She said, "Well, what do I do with these jars, boss?" The prophet basically told her, "What you do now is go out, sell the oil, pay the debt, and you and the kids live on the rest."

God had people out there ready to buy that oil because that's the way God sets us up. This widow didn't know anything about how to get out of her situation, but God endowed her and gave her the practical ability to do it.

It's Not What You Know, but What He Knows

It's not your schooling, status, or ability that's going to prosper you. It is The Blessing that's going to do it! God is not prospering you because of what you know. He is going to prosper you according to what He knows.

The Blessing of Abraham is by grace, and it is on you and me wherever we go. Whatever we lay our hands on is going to prosper. All you've got to do is believe that and obey God, and faith will bring it in!

Conclusion

Y OU HAVE BEEN REDEEMED from poverty, lack, debt, and the limitations this world system has placed on you, through the price Jesus paid for your salvation and freedom. No matter how the economy looks or how much ungodliness becomes accepted by the masses in our society, it won't touch you.

As a citizen in the Kingdom of God, you are operating supernaturally in the new economy that cannot fail. God has called you for such a time as this. Dare to take your place!

Run the Race God Has Set before You

As for us, we have this large crowd of witnesses around us. So then, let us rid ourselves of everything that gets in the way, and of the sin which holds on to us so tightly, and let us run with determination the race that lies before us. Let us keep our eyes fixed on Jesus, on whom our

faith depends from beginning to end. He
did not give up because of the cross! On
the contrary, because of the joy that was
waiting for him, he thought nothing of the
disgrace of dying on the cross, and he is
now seated at the right side of God's throne.
...Have you forgotten the encouraging
words which God speaks to you as his
children?..."My child, pay attention when
the Lord corrects you, and do not be
discouraged when he rebukes you."

—Hebrews 12:1–2, 5 GNT

The next verse (verse 6) says this in the King James Version: "For whom the Lord loveth he chasteneth, and scourgeth every son whom he receiveth." In this verse, *chastening* means "discipline or correction." God doesn't correct you with sickness or trouble. He corrects you in the Spirit. Just as a loving father corrects his child, God corrects you to make you more fruitful and ready to receive every blessing He has for you!

Manifest God's Blessing to the World

What am I doing now? I'm rooting out that unbelief in you. Why? If you want to receive The Blessing of

Abraham and manifest it to the world, you're going to have to have a sense of righteousness: "He made Christ who knew no sin to [judicially] be sin on our behalf, so that in Him we would become the righteousness of God [that is, we would be made acceptable to Him and placed in a right relationship with Him by His gracious lovingkindness]" (2 Corinthians 5:21 AMP).

To fulfill God's divine assignment for your life, you're going to have to know where you stand with Almighty God. He has "made us kings and priests to our God; and we shall reign on the earth" (Revelation 5:10 NKJV).

Prayer for Salvation

Heavenly Father, I come to You in the Name of Your Son, Jesus Christ. You said in Your Word that whosoever shall call upon the Name of the Lord shall be saved (Romans 10:13). Father, I am calling on Jesus right now. I believe He died on the cross for my sins, He was raised from the dead on the third day, and He's alive right now. Lord Jesus, I am asking You now to come into my heart. Live Your life in me and through me. I repent of my sins and surrender myself totally and completely to You. Heavenly Father, by faith I now confess Jesus Christ as my new Lord and Savior and from this day forward, I dedicate my life to serving Him.

Prayer for the Baptism of the Holy Spirit

My Heavenly Father, I am Your child, for I believe in my heart that Jesus has been raised from the dead and I have confessed Him as my Lord. Jesus said, "How much more shall your heavenly Father give the Holy Spirit to them that ask Him" (Luke 11:13). I ask You now in the Name of Jesus to fill me with the Holy Spirit. I step into the fullness and power that I desire in the Name of Jesus. I confess that I am a Spirit-filled Christian. As I yield my vocal organs, I expect to speak in tongues as the Spirit gives me utterance in the Name of Jesus. Praise the Lord! Amen.

Scripture References

- John 14:16–17
- Luke 11:13
- Acts 1:8
- Acts 2:4
- Acts 2:32–33, 38–39
- Acts 8:12–17
- Acts 10:44–46
- Acts 19:2, 5–6
- 1 Corinthians 14:2–15
- 1 Corinthians 14:18, 27
- Ephesians 6:18
- Jude 20

William (Bill) Samuel Winston

B ILL WINSTON IS THE visionary founder and senior pastor of **Living Word Christian Center** in Forest Park, Illinois.

He is also founder and president of **Bill Winston Ministries**, a partnership-based global outreach ministry that shares the gospel through television, radio, and the internet; the nationally accredited **Joseph Business School** which has partnership locations on five continents and an online program; the **Living Word School of Ministry and Missions**; and **Faith Ministries Alliance (FMA)**, an organization

of more than 800 churches and ministries under his spiritual covering in the United States and other countries.

The ministry owns and operates two shopping malls, **Forest Park Plaza** in Forest Park and **Washington Plaza** in Tuskegee, Alabama.

Bill is married to Veronica and is the father of three, Melody, Allegra, and David, and the grandfather of eight.

Books by Bill Winston

- *Be My Witness: Demonstrating the Spirit, Power, and Love of God*
- *Born Again and Spirit-Filled*
- *Climbing without Compromise*
- *Divine Favor — Gift from God, Expanded Edition*
- *Faith and the Marketplace: Becoming the Person of Influence God Intended You to Be, Revised and Expanded Edition*
- *Faith in the Blessing*
- *Imitate God and Get Results*
- *Possessing Your Mountain*
- *Power of the Tongue*
- *Revelation of Royalty: Rediscovering Your Royal Identity in Christ*
- *Seeding for the Billion Flow*
- *Supernatural Wealth Transfer: Restoring the Earth to Its Rightful Owners*
- *Tapping the Wisdom of God*
- *The God Kind of Faith, Expanded Edition*

- *The Kingdom of God in You: Releasing the Kingdom, Replenishing the Earth, Revised and Updated*
- *The Law of Confession: Revolutionize Your Life and Rewrite Your Future with the Power of Words*
- *The Missing Link of Meditation*
- *The Power of Grace*
- *The Power of the Tithe*
- *The Spirit of Leadership: Leadership Lessons Learned from the Life of Joseph*
- *Training for Reigning: Releasing the Power of Your Potential*
- *Transform Your Thinking, Transform Your Life: Radically Change Your Thoughts, Your World, and Your Destiny*
- *Vengeance of the Lord: The Justice System of God*

Some books are available in other languages.

Connect with Us!

CONNECT WITH BILL WINSTON Ministries on social media.

Visit www.billwinston.org/social to connect with all of our official social media channels.

Bill Winston Ministries

P.O. Box 947

Oak Park, Illinois 60303-0947

(708) 697-5100

(800) 711-9327

www.billwinston.org

Bill Winston Ministries Africa

22 Salisbury Road

Morningside, Durban, KWA Zulu Natal 4001

+27(0)313032541

orders@billwinston.org.za www.billwinston.org.za

Bill Winston Ministries Canada

P.O. Box 2900 Vancouver BC V6B 0L4

(844) 298-2900

www.billwinston.ca

Prayer Call Center

(877) 543-9443